Mastering the 'Law of Attraction'

Course Description: Welcome to Mastering the 'Law of Attraction'! This course is designed to provide you with a comprehensive understanding of the 'Law of Attraction' and equip you with practical techniques to manifest your desires and create the life you desire. Throughout this course, you will learn the underlying principles of the 'Law of Attraction', explore various manifestation methods and engage in hands-on exercises to apply these concepts to your daily life. Get ready to harness the power of your thoughts, emotions, and beliefs to manifest your dreams!

Course Duration: Six Weeks

(Can be adjusted as per requirement)

Course Outline

Course Requirements

Week 1: Introduction to the 'Law of Attraction'

- Understanding the 'Law of Attraction' and its core principles
- The role of thoughts, emotions and beliefs in manifestation
- Exploring the power of intention and clarity in attracting what you desire

Week 2: Shifting Mindset and Beliefs

- Identifying and releasing limiting beliefs and negative thought patterns
- Techniques to cultivate a positive and abundant mindset
- Practising gratitude and appreciation as a tool for manifestation

Week 3: Visualisation and Affirmations

- Utilising the power of visualisation to create a clear mental image of your desires
- Crafting effective affirmations and using them to reprogram your subconscious mind
- Designing vision boards and manifestation journals to amplify your manifestation practice

Week 4: Aligning With Vibrations

- Understanding the concept of vibrations and how they influence manifestation
- Techniques to raise your 'Vibrational Frequency' and attract positive experiences

- Harnessing the power of emotions to align with your desires

Week 5: Taking 'Inspired Action'

- Exploring the role of 'action' in the manifestation process
- Distinguishing between 'Inspired Action' and 'Forced Action'
- Developing a plan of action that aligns with your intentions

Week 6: Overcoming Blocks and Challenges

- Identifying and overcoming common blocks to manifestation
- Dealing with doubt, impatience and setbacks along the journey
- Cultivating resilience and maintaining a consistent manifestation practice

Conclusion

Workbook/Journal

Contents

Course Requirements 1
Week 1: Introduction to the 'Law of Attraction' 2
    Lesson 1: Understanding the 'Law of Attraction' and Its Core Principles 2
    Exercise 1: Reflection and Intention Setting 4
    Lesson 2: The Power of Thoughts in Attraction 4
    Exercise 2: The Thought Awareness Practice 5
    Lesson 3: Emotions and Beliefs in Manifestation 6
    Exercise 3: Belief Exploration 7
    Lesson 4: The Power of Clarity and Intention 7
    Exercise 4: Creating a Vision Statement 8
    Lesson 5: 'Law of Attraction' and Daily Practices 8
    Exercise 5: Gratitude Journal 9
    Lesson 6: Review and Recap 10
Week 2: Shifting Mindset and Beliefs 11
    Lesson 1: Identifying and Releasing Limiting Beliefs and Negative Thought Patterns 11
    Exercise 1: Identifying and Challenging Limiting Beliefs 13
    Lesson 2: Techniques to Cultivate a Positive and Abundant Mindset 13
    Exercise 2: Daily Gratitude Practice 14
    Lesson 3: Practising Gratitude and Appreciation as a Tool for Manifestation 15
    Exercise 3: Appreciation Practice 16
    Lesson 4: Recapitulation and Integration 16
Week 3: Visualisation and Affirmations 17
    Lesson 1: The Power of Visualisation in Manifestation 17
    Exercise 1: Guided Visualisation Practice 19
    Lesson 2: Crafting Effective Affirmations for Manifestation 19

    Exercise 2: Crafting Personal Affirmations 21

    Lesson 3: Vision Boards and Manifestation Journals 21

    Exercise 3: Vision Board and Manifestation Journal 22

    Lesson 4: Recapitulation and Integration 22

Week 4: Aligning with Vibrations 23

    Lesson 1: Understanding the Concept of Vibrations in Manifestation 23

    Exercise 1: Self-Reflection on Vibrational Awareness 25

    Lesson 2: Techniques to Raise Your 'Vibrational Frequency' 25

    Exercise 2: Gratitude and High-Vibration Practice 26

    Lesson 3: Harnessing the Power of Emotions to Align with Your Desires 26

    Exercise 3: Emotional Visualisation and Release 27

    Lesson 4: Recapitulation and Integration 28

Week 5: Taking 'Inspired Action' 29

    Lesson 1: The Role of Action in the Manifestation Process 29

    Exercise 1: Reflecting on the Role of Action 30

    Lesson 2: 'Inspired Action' vs 'Forced Action' 31

    Exercise 2: Tuning into Your Inner Guidance 32

    Lesson 3: Developing a Plan of Action 32

    Exercise 3: Creating Your Plan of Action 33

    Lesson 4: Recapitulation and Integration 33

Week 6: Overcoming Blocks and Challenges 34

    Lesson 1: Identifying and Overcoming Common Blocks to Manifestation 35

    Exercise 1: Exploring Limiting Beliefs 35

    Lesson 2: Dealing with Doubt, Impatience and Setbacks 36

    Exercise 2: Building Trust and Patience 36

    Lesson 3: Cultivating Resilience and Maintaining a Consistent Manifestation Practice 37

    Exercise 3: Creating Your Resilience Practice 38

Lesson 4: Recapitulation and Integration 38

Exercise 4: Self-Study Reflection and Planning 39

Conclusion.. 41

WORKBOOK AND JOURNAL 44

WEEK 1 EXERCISES.. 45

Exercise 1: Reflection and Intention Setting.............................. 45

Exercise 2: The Thought Awareness Practice 46

Exercise 3: Belief Exploration 48

Exercise 4: Creating a Vision Statement..................................... 51

Exercise 5: Gratitude Journal 53

WEEK 2 EXERCISES.. 55

Exercise 1: Identifying and Challenging Limiting Beliefs 55

Exercise 2: Daily Gratitude Practice 57

Exercise 3: Appreciation Practice 59

WEEK 3 – EXERCISES 61

Exercise 1: Guided Visualisation Practice 61

Exercise 2: Crafting Personal Affirmations................................. 63

Exercise 3: Vision Board and Manifestation Journal 65

WEEK 4 EXERCISES.. 67

Exercise 1: Self-Reflection on Vibrational Awareness 67

Exercise 2: Gratitude and High Vibration Practice 69

Exercise 3: Emotional Visualisation and Release 71

WEEK 5 EXERCISES.. 73

Exercise 1: Reflecting on the Role of Action 73

Exercise 2: Tuning into Your Inner Guidance............................ 75

Exercise 3: Creating Your Plan of Action 77

WEEK 6: EXERCISES.. 79

Exercise 1: Exploring Limiting Beliefs... 79

Exercise 2: Building Trust and Patience 81

Exercise 3: Creating Your Resilience Practice.......................... 83

Exercise 4: Self-Study Reflection and Planning 85

Course Requirements

- A journal or notebook for exercises and reflections. (We have attached a journal to the course but you may prefer to use your own.)
- An open mind and willingness to explore new concepts.
- Dedication and commitment to practising the techniques regularly.

By the end of this course, you will have a deep understanding of the 'Law of Attraction' and the ability to manifest your desires effectively. You will have developed practical skills and techniques to align your thoughts, beliefs and actions with your intentions, enabling you to create the life you envision. Get ready to unlock your manifesting potential and embark on a transformative journey!

Week 1: Introduction to the 'Law of Attraction'

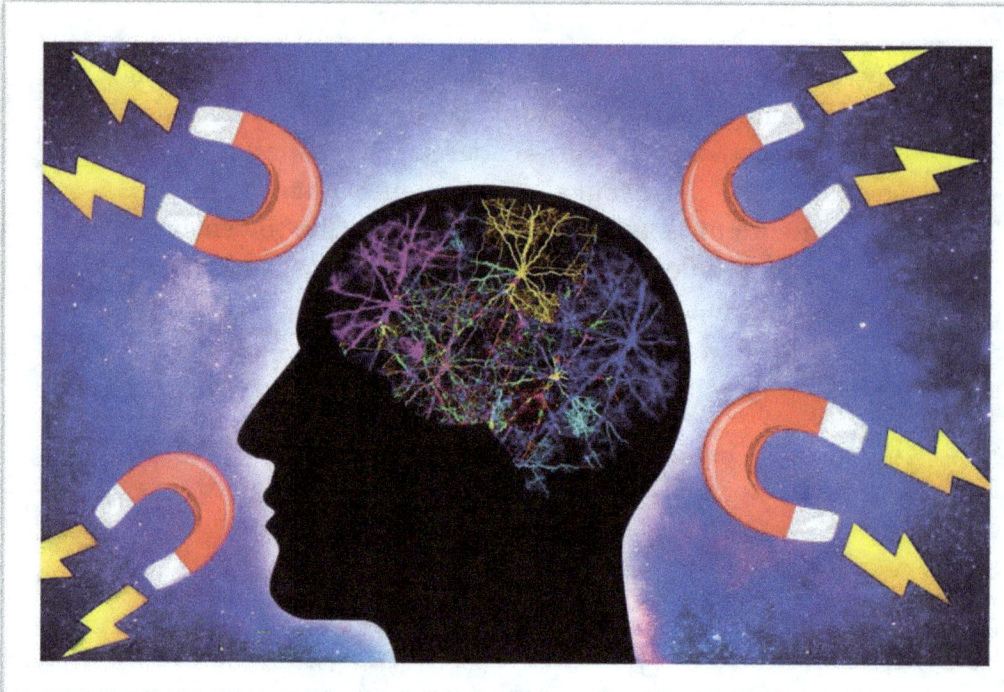

Lesson 1: Understanding the 'Law of Attraction' and Its Core Principles

In this lesson, we will explore the fundamental principles of the 'Law of Attraction' and how it shapes our reality.
Definition and Explanation of the 'Law of Attraction': It states that like attracts like. It suggests that our thoughts, emotions and beliefs have the power to attract corresponding experiences into our lives. In essence, we create our reality through the energetic vibrations we emit.

The Principle of Like Attracts Like: According to the 'Law of Attraction', similar energy vibrations are drawn to each other. Positive thoughts and emotions attract positive experiences, while negative thoughts and emotions attract negative experiences. By understanding and aligning with this principle, we can consciously manifest our desires.

The Role of Thoughts, Emotions, and Beliefs in Manifestation: Our thoughts, emotions, and beliefs are powerful energetic forces that influence what we attract into our lives. Positive thoughts, emotions and empowering beliefs create a magnetic field of attraction for the things we desire. Conversely, negative thoughts, emotions and limiting beliefs can block the manifestation process.

The Connection Between Vibration and Attraction: Everything in the universe vibrates at a specific frequency, including our thoughts and emotions. The 'Law of Attraction' teaches us that we attract experiences and circumstances that vibrate at a similar frequency to our dominant thoughts and emotions. By consciously raising our 'Vibrational Frequency', we can align ourselves with positive outcomes.

Exercise 1: Reflection and Intention Setting

Take some time to reflect on your current beliefs and thoughts about the 'Law of Attraction'. Write down your understanding of it and any preconceived notions you may have. Set an intention for this course, specifying what you hope to manifest and experience by the end of it.

Lesson 2: The Power of Thoughts in Attraction

In this lesson, we will delve into the impact of our thoughts on the manifestation process and learn techniques to shift away from negative thought patterns.

Understanding the Relationship Between 'Thoughts' and 'Reality': Our thoughts are not merely random occurrences but potent creators of our reality. What we consistently think about and focus on shapes our experiences. By becoming aware of our thought patterns, we can actively shape our reality.

How 'Negative Thoughts' and 'Self-Talk' Can Hinder 'Manifestation': Negative thoughts and self-talk act as powerful barriers to manifestation. When we constantly dwell on self-doubt, fear and inadequacy, we send out vibrations that attract unwanted circumstances. Recognising and transforming negative thoughts is crucial for successful manifestation.

Techniques for Shifting Negative Thought Patterns to Positive Ones:

a. Affirmations: These are positive statements that counteract negative thoughts. By repeating empowering affirmations, we reprogram our subconscious mind and align our thoughts with our desires.

b. Reframing: This involves consciously shifting our perspective on challenging situations or negative thoughts. By finding positive aspects or lessons in seemingly negative experiences, we can transform our mindset.

Exercise 2: The Thought Awareness Practice

Throughout the week, pay close attention to your thoughts. Whenever you notice a negative or limiting thought, pause and replace it with a positive affirmation or thought that aligns with your desires. Keep a record of these thoughts and affirmations in your journal.

Lesson 3: Emotions & Beliefs in Manifestation

In this lesson, we will explore the crucial role of emotions and beliefs in the manifestation process and learn techniques to cultivate positive emotional states.

The Impact of Emotions on Manifestation: Emotions are powerful indicators of our 'Vibrational Frequency' and play a significant role in the manifestation process. Positive emotions like joy, love, and gratitude increase our 'Vibrational Frequency', attracting experiences aligned with those emotions. Negative emotions such as fear, doubt and anger lower our frequency and hinder manifestation.

Identifying Limiting Beliefs and Releasing Them: Limiting beliefs are deeply ingrained thoughts or perceptions that restrict us from achieving our desires. By identifying and challenging these beliefs, we can replace them with empowering ones that support our manifestation journey.
Cultivating Positive Emotions to Align With Your Desires:

a. Gratitude Practice: Expressing gratitude for what we already have raises our 'Vibrational Frequency' and opens the door to more abundance. Cultivate a daily gratitude practice to enhance your manifestation process.
b. Emotional Visualisation: Engage in visualising and feeling the emotions associated with already having manifested your

desires. By immersing yourself in these positive emotions, you align yourself with the vibration of your desires.

Exercise 3: Belief Exploration

Reflect on your beliefs about your ability to manifest your desires. Identify any limiting beliefs that may be holding you back. Write them down and challenge them by finding evidence or alternative beliefs that support your manifestation journey.

Lesson 4: The Power of Clarity and Intention

This lesson focuses on the significance of setting clear intentions and gaining clarity about what you want to manifest.

Setting Clear and Specific Intentions for Manifestation: Intentions act as the compass that directs our manifestation efforts. When we have a clear and specific intention, we provide the universe with a focused target for manifestation.

The Importance of Knowing What You Want and Why: Clarity about what we want and why we want it is vital for successful manifestation. When we understand our desires at a deep level and connect them with our values and passions, our intentions become more powerful.

Techniques for Gaining Clarity on Your Desires:

a. Journaling: Engage in journaling exercises to explore your desires, values, and aspirations. Write freely about what you want to manifest and how it aligns with your life purpose.
b. Visualisation: Visualise yourself already living your desired reality in vivid detail. Allow yourself to feel the emotions associated with your manifestation. This practice helps to clarify your desires and strengthens your intention.

Exercise 4: Creating a Vision Statement

Write a detailed vision statement that encapsulates your desires. Be specific and vivid in describing what you want to manifest. Visualise yourself already experiencing it as you write. Keep this vision statement in a prominent place as a reminder of your intentions.

Lesson 5: 'Law of Attraction' and Daily Practices

This lesson emphasises integrating the 'Law of Attraction' into your daily life through rituals and practices that reinforce manifestation.

Integrating the 'Law of Attraction' into Your Daily Life: Manifestation is not a one-time event; it is a continuous process. By incorporating the 'Law of Attraction' into your daily routine, you keep your focus on your desires and maintain a high 'Vibrational Frequency'.

Rituals and Practices to Reinforce Manifestation:

a. Affirmations and Visualisation: Practise affirmations and visualisation techniques daily to reinforce positive beliefs and keep your desires at the forefront of your mind.
b. Meditation and Mindfulness: Engage in meditation and mindfulness practices to quieten the mind, reduce resistance and enhance your ability to receive guidance from the universe.
c. Act As If: Behave and act as if you have already manifested your desires. This practice helps you align your thoughts, emotions and actions with your intentions.
Incorporating Gratitude and Appreciation into Your Routine: Gratitude and appreciation amplify the manifestation process. Take time each day to express gratitude for what you have already manifested and the abundance in your life.

Exercise 5: Gratitude Journal

Start a gratitude journal and make it a daily practice to write down at least three things you are grateful for. Reflect on the positive aspects of your life and the things you are already manifesting. This practice will help shift your focus towards abundance and attract more of it.

Lesson 6: Review and Recap

In the final lesson of the week, go over the core concepts covered during the week.

Note: Practise the exercises regularly throughout the week and document your experiences, insights and any challenges faced in your journals. Building a strong foundation in the fundamentals of the 'Law of Attraction' is crucial for successful manifestation.

Week 2: Shifting Mindset and Beliefs

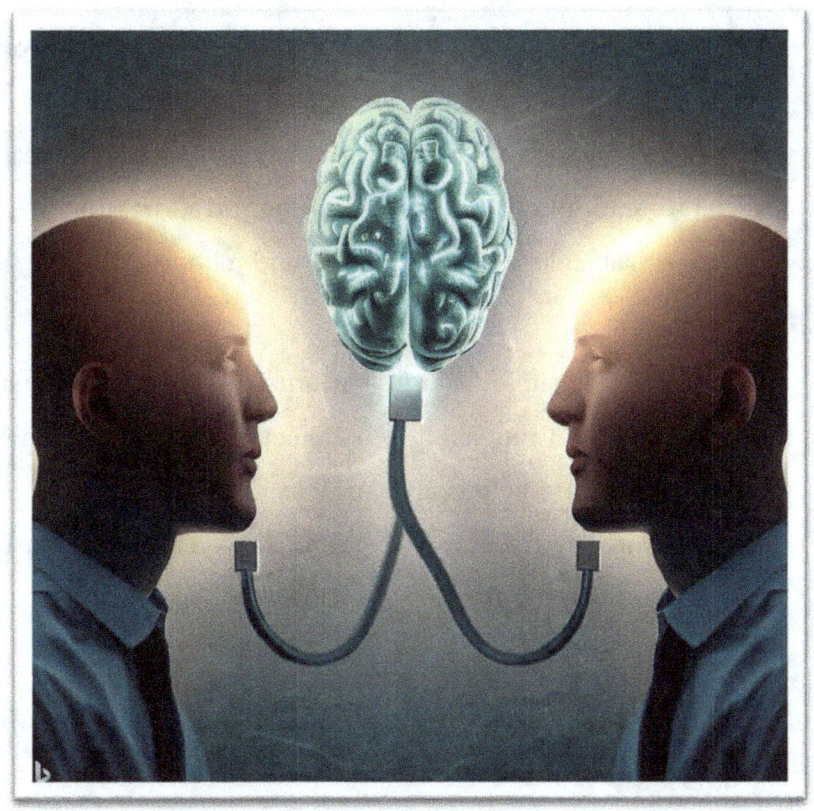

Lesson 1: Identifying and Releasing Limiting Beliefs and Negative Thought Patterns

In this lesson, we will focus on recognising and releasing the limiting beliefs and negative thought patterns that hinder our manifestation efforts.

Understanding Limiting Beliefs: Limiting beliefs are deeply ingrained thoughts and perceptions that hold us back from achieving our desires. They often stem from past experiences, societal conditioning or fear. Identifying and addressing these beliefs is crucial for personal growth and manifestation.

Recognising Negative Thought Patterns: They can be habitual and automatic, influencing our perception of reality. They reinforce limiting beliefs and attract unwanted experiences. By becoming aware of these patterns, we can consciously choose empowering thoughts.

Techniques for Releasing Limiting Beliefs and Negative Thought Patterns:

a. Self-Reflection: Engage in self-reflection to identify recurring negative thoughts and underlying beliefs. Challenge their validity and replace them with empowering alternatives.

b. Affirmations and Positive Self-Talk: Utilise these to counteract negative thoughts and rewire your subconscious mind.

c. EFT (emotional freedom technique): It involves tapping on specific acupressure points while repeating affirmations in order to release negative emotions and beliefs.

d. Journaling: Write down your limiting beliefs and negative thought patterns; challenge their validity and replace them with positive and empowering beliefs.

Exercise 1: Identifying and Challenging Limiting Beliefs

Identify at least three limiting beliefs that you hold about yourself, your abilities or your potential for manifestation. Write them down in your journal and challenge their validity. Generate empowering beliefs that align with your desires and that replace the limiting beliefs.

Lesson 2: Techniques to Cultivate a Positive and Abundant Mindset

In this lesson, we will explore techniques to cultivate a positive and abundant mindset, which is crucial for successful manifestation.

Mindfulness and Awareness: Practising mindfulness and cultivating present-moment awareness helps us to observe our thoughts and emotions without judgment. This awareness allows us to consciously choose positive thoughts and emotions that align with our desires.

Positive Visualisation: Engaging in positive visualisation exercises helps to create a mental image of the reality you wish to manifest. Visualise yourself already experiencing your desires and feel the positive emotions associated with it. This practice reinforces a positive mindset.

Gratitude and Appreciation: Gratitude is a powerful tool for shifting our mindset and attracting more abundance. Cultivating gratitude and appreciating the blessings in our lives increases our 'Vibrational Frequency' and opens the door for more positive experiences.

Surrounding Yourself with Positivity: Surround yourself with positive influences, whether they be uplifting books, inspiring people, or supportive communities. Positive environments and associations contribute to a positive mindset.

Exercise 2: Daily Gratitude Practice

Commit to a daily gratitude practice. Each day, write down three things you are grateful for in your journal. Reflect on the positive aspects of your life and the progress you are making towards manifesting your desires. Feel the genuine appreciation for these blessings.

Lesson 3: Practising Gratitude and Appreciation as a Tool for Manifestation

In this lesson, we will delve deeper into the power of gratitude and appreciation as tools for manifestation.

The Role of Gratitude in Manifestation: Gratitude is a magnet for abundance. When we express gratitude for what we already have, we send a powerful message to the universe that we are open to receiving more.

The Practice of Appreciation: It goes beyond gratitude. It involves fully recognising and cherishing the positive aspects of our lives. By consciously appreciating the present moment and all its blessings, we shift our focus to abundance.
Techniques to Enhance Gratitude and Appreciation:

a. Gratitude Journal: Maintain a gratitude journal in which you regularly write down the things you are grateful for. This practice helps shift your mindset towards positivity and abundance.

b. Gratitude Rituals: Say a gratitude prayer before meals or express appreciation before bedtime, for example. These rituals deepen your connection to gratitude.

Exercise 3: Appreciation Practice

Choose one aspect of your life, or an experience that you deeply appreciate. Write a letter expressing your appreciation and gratitude for it. Read the letter aloud, allowing yourself to feel the genuine emotions associated with appreciation.

Lesson 4: Recapitulation and Integration

In this lesson, we will review and integrate the concepts and practices covered during the week. We will address any questions or concerns and provide additional resources for further exploration.

Note: Practise the exercises regularly throughout the week and document your experiences, insights, and any challenges faced in your journals. Consistency is important in shifting mindset and beliefs for successful manifestation.

Week 3: Visualisation and Affirmations

Lesson 1: The Power of Visualisation in Manifestation

In this lesson, we will explore the practice of visualisation and how it can help create a clear mental image of your desires.

Understanding Visualisation: It is the process of creating detailed mental images of your desires. By vividly imagining and feeling the experience of already having what you want, you align your energy with your desires and attract them into your reality.

Benefits of Visualisation:

a. Clarifying Your Desires: Visualisation helps you gain clarity about what you truly want to manifest.

b. Amplifying Emotional Alignment: By immersing yourself in the emotions associated with your desires, you increase your 'Vibrational Frequency' and attract corresponding experiences.

c. Enhancing Belief and Confidence: Visualisation reinforces your belief in the possibility of your desires, boosting your confidence in the manifestation process.

Techniques for Effective Visualisation:

a. Guided Visualisation: Use pre-recorded guided visualisation audios or videos to assist you in creating detailed mental images of your desires.

b. Creative Visualisation: Engage your senses to make the visualisation experience more vivid and realistic. Imagine the sights, sounds, smells, tastes and textures associated with your desires.

Exercise 1: Guided Visualisation Practice

Find a quiet and comfortable space where you will not be interrupted. Listen to a guided visualisation audio or video that aligns with your desired manifestation. Follow the instructions and immerse yourself in the experience, allowing yourself to feel the emotions associated with already having your desires.

Lesson 2: Crafting Effective Affirmations for Manifestation

In this lesson, we will explore the power of affirmations and how to craft effective ones that support your manifestation journey.

Understanding Affirmations: They are positive statements that reinforce empowering beliefs and thoughts. By repetitively stating affirmations, you reprogram your subconscious mind and align your thoughts with your desires.

Qualities of Effective Affirmations:

a. Present Tense: Phrase your affirmations as if you already have what you desire. This creates a sense of immediacy and reinforces the belief that your desires are already manifesting.

b. Positive Language: Use positive and empowering language in your affirmations. Focus on what you want to attract, rather than what you want to avoid.

c. Emotional Connection: Infuse your affirmations with the emotions associated with already having your desires. This amplifies their impact.

Techniques for Using Affirmations:

a. Repetition: Repeat your affirmations regularly, preferably multiple times a day. Consistency is the key to rewiring your subconscious mind.

b. Visualisation and Emotion: Combine affirmations with visualisation. While stating your affirmations, imagine yourself already living your desired reality, and feel the positive emotions associated with it.

Exercise 2: Crafting Personal Affirmations

Write at least five personal affirmations that align with your desires. Ensure they meet the criteria of being in the present tense, positive and emotionally connected. Practise saying these affirmations aloud daily, preferably in front of a mirror, and feel the power of their positive impact.

Lesson 3: Vision Boards and Manifestation Journals

In this lesson, we will explore the use of vision boards and manifestation journals as powerful tools to amplify your manifestation practice.

Vision Boards:

a. Creating a Vision Board: Gather images, words, and symbols that represent your desires. Arrange them on a vision board, either physically or digitally, in a way that evokes positive emotions and a clear visualisation of your desired reality. b. Placing Your Attention: Regularly spend time looking at your vision board and visualising yourself already living the experiences depicted. This reinforces your focus and intention.

Manifestation Journals:

a. Designing Your Manifestation Journal: Create a dedicated journal in which you record your manifestations, progress and insights. Use it to write affirmations, visualise and reflect on your desires.

b. Daily Practice: Make it a habit to write in your manifestation journal every day. Include your gratitude list, affirmations, visualisations and any 'Inspired Actions' you take towards your desires.

Exercise 3: Vision Board and Manifestation Journal

Create a vision board that represents your desires. Collect images, words and symbols that resonate with your goals and arrange them on your vision board. Place your vision board in a prominent place where you can see it daily. Additionally, start your manifestation journal and write down your affirmations, visualisations and reflections on your desires.

Lesson 4: Recapitulation and Integration

In this lesson, we will review the concepts and practices covered during the week.

Note: Practise visualisation and affirmations regularly throughout the week. Engage with your vision boards and manifestation journals on a daily basis, reinforcing your desires and maintaining a positive mindset.

Week 4: Aligning with Vibrations

Lesson 1: Understanding the Concept of Vibrations in Manifestation

In this lesson, we will explore the concept of vibrations and how they influence the manifestation process.

The Law of Vibration: According to this law, everything in the universe is made up of energy and emits its own unique vibration. This includes our thoughts, emotions and desires. Understanding this concept allows us to consciously align our vibrations with what we want to manifest.

'Vibrational Frequency': Each person and object has one; it is the energetic signature they emit. Our 'Vibrational Frequency' determines what we attract into our lives. By raising it, we can align with positive experiences and manifest our desires effortlessly.

The Role of Vibrations in Manifestation: Our thoughts, emotions, and beliefs emit vibrations that interact with the energetic field of the universe. By aligning our vibrations with our desires, we send out a clear and powerful signal to the universe, attracting experiences that match our 'Vibrational Frequency'.

Exercise 1: Self-Reflection on Vibrational Awareness

Reflect on your own vibrational awareness. Consider how your thoughts, emotions, and beliefs may be affecting your 'Vibrational Frequency' and manifestation efforts. Write down any insights or observations in your journal.

Lesson 2: Techniques to Raise Your 'Vibrational Frequency'

In this lesson, we will explore techniques to raise your 'Vibrational Frequency' and attract positive experiences into your life.

Positive Affirmations and Self-Talk: Utilise these to shift your mindset and raise your 'Vibrational Frequency'. Repeat affirmations that resonate with your desires and reinforce positive beliefs about yourself and your manifestations.

Gratitude and Appreciation: Cultivate a practice of gratitude and appreciation to raise your 'Vibrational Frequency'. Regularly acknowledge and express gratitude for the blessings, opportunities, and experiences in your life. This practice helps shift your focus towards positivity and abundance.

Surrounding Yourself with High Vibrational Energy: Surround yourself with people, environments and activities that uplift and inspire you. Engage in hobbies, practices, and conversations that bring you joy and align with your desires. This helps to raise your 'Vibrational Frequency' by absorbing the positive energy around you.

Exercise 2: Gratitude and High-Vibration Practice

Take a few minutes each day to write down three things you are grateful for in your manifestation journal. Engage in an activity or spend time with someone who brings you joy and raises your 'Vibrational Frequency'. Notice the impact on your overall energy and mindset.

Lesson 3: Harnessing the Power of Emotions to Align with Your Desires

In this lesson, we will explore the power of emotions in aligning with your desires and manifesting effectively.

Emotions as Indicators: Emotions are powerful indicators of our 'Vibrational Frequency'. Positive emotions such as joy, love and enthusiasm indicate alignment with our desires, while negative emotions like fear, doubt and frustration signify a misalignment. Paying attention to your emotions helps you course-correct and align with your desires.

Emotional Visualisation: Engage in emotional visualisation exercises to amplify your alignment with your desires. While visualising, focus not just on the images but also on the positive emotions associated with achieving your desires. Feel the joy, gratitude, and excitement as if it has already happened.

Emotional Release and Healing: Release any negative emotions or energetic blocks that may be hindering your manifestation efforts. Practise techniques such as meditation, deep breathing, or energy healing modalities to release and heal any emotional wounds or limiting beliefs.

Exercise 3: Emotional Visualisation and Release

Engage in an emotional visualisation practice where you vividly imagine yourself living your desired reality. Feel the positive emotions associated with the manifestation. Additionally, spend time journaling about any negative emotions or limiting beliefs that may be holding you back. Explore techniques such as meditation or energy healing to release and heal these emotions.

Lesson 4: Recapitulation and Integration

Review and integrate the concepts and practices covered during the week.

Note: Practise raising your 'Vibrational Frequency' regularly throughout the week. Self-awareness and emotional alignment are important components of the manifestation process. Document your experiences and any shifts in their 'Vibrational Frequency' in your manifestation journals.

Week 5: Taking 'Inspired Action'

Lesson 1: The Role of Action in the Manifestation Process

In this lesson, we will explore the importance of taking action in the manifestation process and how it contributes to the realisation of your desires.

Action as a Catalyst: While thoughts, emotions, and vibrations play a significant role in manifesting, action acts as a catalyst that brings your desires into physical reality. Taking 'Inspired Action' is an essential component of the manifestation process.

Alignment with Intentions: Action must be aligned with your intentions and desires to create meaningful progress. It is through intentional and purposeful actions that you demonstrate your commitment and belief in the manifestation of your desires.

Co-creation with the Universe: Taking action shows the universe that you are ready and willing to participate in co-creating your reality. It opens up doors of opportunities and allows for synchronicities and serendipitous events to occur.

Exercise 1: Reflecting on the Role of Action

Reflect on the role of action in your manifestation journey. Consider the actions you have taken so far and how they have contributed to your progress. Write down any insights or observations in your journal.

Lesson 2: 'Inspired Action' vs 'Forced Action'

In this lesson, we will distinguish between 'Inspired Action' and 'Forced Action' and understand the significance of taking action from a place of alignment and intuition.

'Inspired Action': This arises naturally from a place of alignment with your desires. It is driven by intuition, inspiration and inner guidance. 'Inspired Action' feels effortless, joyful and in flow.

'Forced Action': This, on the other hand, stems from a sense of obligation, external pressure or fear. It feels forced, resistant and disconnected from your true desires. 'Forced Action' often leads to frustration and limited results.

Listening to Your Inner Guidance: Developing the ability to listen to your inner guidance and intuition is crucial in discerning between inspired and 'Forced Action'. Tuning into your intuition allows you to take actions that are in alignment with your highest good.

Exercise 2: Tuning into Your Inner Guidance

Practise tuning into your inner guidance by engaging in meditation or quiet reflection. Ask yourself questions related to your desires and listen for intuitive nudges or insights. Pay attention to any inspired ideas or actions that arise from this practice.

Lesson 3: Developing a Plan of Action

In this lesson, we will focus on developing a plan of action that aligns with your intentions and supports the manifestation of your desires.

Clarity of Intentions: Before creating a plan of action, it is essential to have clarity about your intentions and what you want to manifest. Clearly define your goals and desires to guide your action steps effectively.

Prioritising Actions: Identify the actions that will have the greatest impact on manifesting your desires. Prioritise these actions based on their alignment with your intentions and their potential to move you closer to your desired outcomes.

Flexibility and Adaptability: While a plan of action is important, it is equally important to remain flexible and adaptable. Be open to unexpected opportunities, course corrections and new insights that may arise along the way.

Exercise 3: Creating Your Plan of Action

Create a plan of action that outlines the key steps you need to take to manifest your desires. Break down these steps into smaller, manageable tasks and assign timelines to each. Ensure that each action is aligned with your intentions and feels inspiring and in alignment with your true desires.

Lesson 4: Recapitulation and Integration

In this final lesson of the course, we will review and integrate the concepts and practices covered throughout the course. We will address any questions or concerns and provide additional resources for further exploration.

Note: Take 'Inspired Action' regularly throughout the week. Alignment, intuition and flexibility are important in your action-taking process. Document your action steps, progress, and any synchronicities or unexpected opportunities that arise as a result of your 'Inspired Actions'.

Week 6: Overcoming Blocks and Challenges

Lesson 1: Identifying and Overcoming Common Blocks to Manifestation

In this lesson, we will explore common blocks that can hinder the manifestation process and techniques to overcome them.

Limiting Beliefs and Self-Sabotage: Identify and address any limiting beliefs that may be holding you back from manifesting your desires. Learn techniques to reframe negative thoughts and beliefs into empowering ones.

Fear and Resistance: Recognise and confront any fears or resistance that may arise when pursuing your manifestations. Develop strategies to work through fear and resistance, allowing you to move forward with confidence.

External Influences: Identify any external influences or negative energies that may be affecting your manifestation efforts. Learn how to protect your energy, set boundaries, and surround yourself with supportive and positive influences.

Exercise 1: Exploring Limiting Beliefs

Take some time to reflect on any limiting beliefs that may be blocking your manifestations. Write them down in your manifestation journal and then challenge each belief by providing evidence to the contrary. Replace these limiting beliefs with empowering affirmations.

Lesson 2: Dealing with Doubt, Impatience and Setbacks

In this lesson, we will address doubt, impatience and setbacks that may arise during the manifestation journey and learn strategies to overcome them.

Cultivating Trust and Faith: Develop trust in the universe and faith in the manifestation process. Remind yourself of past manifestations or positive experiences that can reinforce your belief in the power of manifestation.

Patience and Surrender: Practise patience and surrender to the timing of the universe. Understand that the manifestation process unfolds in its own time, and trust that everything is working out for your highest good.

Learning from Setbacks: View setbacks as opportunities for growth and learning. Analyse setbacks to gain insights and make adjustments to your approach. Remember that setbacks do not define your ability to manifest.

Exercise 2: Building Trust and Patience

Engage in activities that cultivate trust and patience within you. Practise meditation or visualisation exercises to strengthen your faith in the manifestation process. Write down affirmations that reinforce your trust and patience, and read them daily.

Lesson 3: Cultivating Resilience and Maintaining a Consistent Manifestation Practice

In this lesson, we will focus on cultivating resilience and maintaining a consistent manifestation practice, even in the face of challenges.

Self-Care and Well-being: Prioritise self-care and well-being to support your manifestation practice. Take care of your physical, mental and emotional health, as they directly impact your ability to manifest effectively.

Daily Rituals and Practices: Develop daily rituals and practices that keep you connected to your desires, and maintain a high 'Vibrational Frequency'. This can include meditation, visualisation, journaling or affirmations.

Community and Support: Surround yourself with a supportive community or find a manifestation buddy who can provide encouragement and accountability. Share your manifestations and challenges with like-minded individuals who can offer guidance and support.

Exercise 3: Creating Your Resilience Practice

Design a resilience practice that aligns with your needs and preferences. This can include activities like exercise, mindfulness, gratitude or any other practices that help you cultivate resilience. Integrate this practice into your daily routine.

Lesson 4: Recapitulation and Integration

In this final lesson of the course, you will take the opportunity to recapitulate and integrate the concepts and practices covered throughout the course into your self-study journey.

Reviewing Course Material: Take time to review the course material, including lecture notes, exercises and any additional resources provided. Reflect on your understanding of the concepts and identify any areas that require further clarification.

Self-Reflection and Application: Engage in self-reflection by journaling about your experiences and observations during the course. Consider how the lessons and exercises have impacted your mindset, beliefs and manifestation practice. Apply the knowledge gained to your own life and manifestations.

Seeking Additional Resources: As part of self-study, explore additional resources such as books, articles, podcasts or videos on the 'Law of Attraction' and manifestation. Expand your understanding and gather a range of perspectives to deepen your knowledge.

Implementing Consistent Practice: Commit to a consistent manifestation practice that aligns with your personal preferences and schedule. Design a routine that incorporates techniques like visualisation, affirmations, gratitude or meditation. Dedicate time each day to nurture your manifestation journey.

Tracking Your Progress: Create a progress tracker or journal to document your manifestations, insights and growth over time. Regularly review and celebrate your successes to reinforce positive momentum and maintain motivation.

Exercise 4: Self-Study Reflection and Planning

Allocate dedicated time for self-reflection and planning. Set aside uninterrupted moments to review the course material, engage in journaling exercises and plan your ongoing self-study journey. Consider how you will incorporate the lessons and practices into your daily life.

Note: As you engage in self-study, remember to be patient and kind to yourself. Embrace the journey as a continuous learning process, allowing for experimentation and growth. Seek support from online communities, forums or discussion groups to connect with like-minded individuals and share your experiences.

Conclusion

Congratulations on completing 'Mastering the "Law of Attraction" '! Over the past weeks, you have embarked on a transformative journey, diving deep into the principles and practices of the 'Law of Attraction'. As you wrap up this course, take a moment to acknowledge your commitment to personal growth and your dedication to **manifesting a life filled with abundance, joy, and fulfilment.**

Throughout the course, you have gained valuable insights into the power of your thoughts, emotions, beliefs and actions in shaping your reality. You have learned to align your vibrations with your desires, cultivate a positive mindset and overcome blocks and challenges along the way. By harnessing the 'Law of Attraction', you have unlocked your potential to create a life that resonates with your deepest aspirations and desires.

Remember, the journey of manifestation does not end here. It is a lifelong practice that requires consistent effort, self-reflection and belief in your own power to co-create with the universe. Embrace the lessons and tools you have learned in this course and continue to integrate them into your daily life. As you move forward, be open to new possibilities, embrace the power of gratitude, and listen to your intuition as it guides you toward 'Inspired Action'. Trust in the process, knowing that the universe is conspiring and aligning itself in your favour.

Celebrate your accomplishments, big and small, and use them as steppingstones towards even greater manifestations. Surround yourself with a supportive community that uplifts and encourages you on your journey. Remember that you are not alone; there are countless individuals who are also on their path to manifesting their dreams.

As we conclude this course, I invite you to take a moment to reflect on how far you have come on this life-transforming journey. Acknowledge the shifts in your mindset, the growth in your beliefs and the transformation in your actions. Trust that you have the tools and knowledge to continue manifesting your desires and creating a life of abundance and fulfilment.

Remember, you have the power to manifest the life you desire. Embrace the 'Law of Attraction' as a guiding force in your journey and allow it to shape your reality in extraordinary ways. Trust in the magic of the universe and believe in the limitless possibilities that await you.

May your manifestations be abundant, your vibrations be high and your journey be filled with joy and fulfilment.

Congratulations once again, and may your future be filled with the manifestations of your dreams!

Wishing you continued success and happiness on your manifestation journey!

With gratitude,
Tariq S.

Note: The 'Law of Attraction' is a belief system, and its effectiveness can vary from person to person. This course aims to provide guidance and tools based on popular concepts related to the 'Law of Attraction' but does not guarantee specific outcomes.

WORKBOOK AND JOURNAL

WEEK 1 EXERCISES

Exercise 1: Reflection and Intention Setting

Take some time to reflect on your current beliefs and thoughts about the 'Law of Attraction'. Write down your understanding of it any preconceived notions you may have. Set an intention for this course, specifying what you hope to manifest and experience by the end of it.

_____
_____
_____
_____
_____
_____
_____
_____
_____
_____
_____
_____
_____
_____
_____

Exercise 2: The Thought Awareness Practice

Throughout the week, pay close attention to your thoughts. Whenever you notice a negative or limiting thought, pause and replace it with a positive affirmation or thought that aligns with your desires. Keep a record of these thoughts and affirmations in your journal.

_____
_____
_____
_____
_____
_____
_____
_____
_____
_____
_____
_____
_____
_____
_____
_____
_____

Exercise 3: Belief Exploration

Reflect on your beliefs about your ability to manifest your desires. Identify any limiting beliefs that may be holding you back. Write them down and challenge them by finding evidence or alternative beliefs that support your manifestation journey.

_____
_____
_____
_____
_____
_____
_____
_____
_____
_____
_____
_____
_____
_____
_____
_____
_____

Exercise 4: Creating a Vision Statement

Write a detailed vision statement that encapsulates your desires. Be specific and vivid in describing what you want to manifest. Visualise yourself already experiencing it as you write. Keep this vision statement in a prominent place as a reminder of your intentions.

_____

_____

_____

_____

_____

_____

_____

_____

_____

_____

_____

_____

_____

_____

_____

_____

Exercise 5: Gratitude Journal

Start a gratitude journal and make it a daily practice to write down at least three things you are grateful for. Reflect on the positive aspects of your life and the things you are already manifesting. This practice will help shift your focus towards abundance and attract more of it.

_____
_____
_____
_____
_____
_____
_____
_____
_____
_____
_____
_____
_____
_____
_____

WEEK 2 EXERCISES

Exercise 1: Identifying and Challenging Limiting Beliefs

Identify at least three limiting beliefs that you hold about yourself, your abilities or your potential for manifestation. Write them down in your journal and challenge their validity. Generate empowering beliefs that align with your desires and that replace the limiting beliefs.

_____
_____
_____
_____
_____
_____
_____
_____
_____
_____
_____
_____
_____
_____

Exercise 2: Daily Gratitude Practice

Commit to a daily gratitude practice. Each day, write down three things you are grateful for in your journal. Reflect on the positive aspects of your life and the progress you are making towards manifesting your desires. Feel genuine appreciation for these blessings.

_____

_____

_____

_____

_____

_____

_____

_____

_____

_____

_____

_____

_____

_____

_____

Exercise 3: Appreciation Practice

Choose one aspect of your life or an experience that you deeply appreciate. Write a letter expressing your appreciation and gratitude for it. Read the letter aloud, allowing yourself to feel the genuine emotions associated with appreciation.

WEEK 3 – EXERCISES

Exercise 1: Guided Visualisation Practice

Find a quiet and comfortable space where you won't be interrupted. Listen to a guided visualisation audio or video that aligns with your desired manifestation. Follow the instructions and immerse yourself in the experience, allowing yourself to feel the emotions associated with already having your desires.

_____
_____
_____
_____
_____
_____
_____
_____
_____
_____
_____
_____
_____

Exercise 2: Crafting Personal Affirmations

Write at least five personal affirmations that align with your desires. Ensure they meet the criteria of being in the present tense, positive and emotionally connected. Practise saying these affirmations aloud daily—preferably in front of a mirror—and feel the power of their positive impact.

_____
_____
_____
_____
_____
_____
_____
_____
_____
_____
_____
_____
_____
_____
_____
_____
_____

Exercise 3: Vision Board and Manifestation Journal

Create a vision board that represents your desires. Collect images, words and symbols that resonate with your goals, and arrange them on your vision board. Place your vision board in a prominent place where you can see it daily. Additionally, start your manifestation journal and write down your affirmations and visualisations, as well as your reflections on your desires.

_____

_____

_____

_____

_____

_____

_____

_____

_____

_____

_____

_____

WEEK 4 EXERCISES

Exercise 1: Self-Reflection on Vibrational Awareness

Reflect on your own vibrational awareness. Consider how your thoughts, emotions, and beliefs may be affecting your 'Vibrational Frequency' and manifestation efforts. Write down any insights or observations in your journal.

_____
_____
_____
_____
_____
_____
_____
_____
_____
_____
_____
_____
_____
_____
_____

Exercise 2: Gratitude and High Vibration Practice

Take a few minutes each day to write down three things you are grateful for in your manifestation journal. Engage in an activity, or spend time with someone who brings you joy and raises your 'Vibrational Frequency'. Notice the impact on your overall energy and mindset.

_____

_____

_____

_____

_____

_____

_____

_____

_____

_____

_____

_____

_____

_____

_____

Exercise 3: Emotional Visualisation and Release

Engage in an emotional visualisation practice in which you vividly imagine yourself living your desired reality. Feel the positive emotions associated with the manifestation. Additionally, spend time journaling about any negative emotions or limiting beliefs that may be holding you back. Explore techniques such as meditation or energy healing to release and heal these emotions.

_____
_____
_____
_____
_____
_____
_____
_____
_____
_____
_____
_____
_____

WEEK 5 EXERCISES

Exercise 1: Reflecting on the Role of Action

Reflect on the role of action in your manifestation journey. Consider the actions you have taken so far and how they have contributed to your progress. Write down any insights or observations in your journal.

_____
_____
_____
_____
_____
_____
_____
_____
_____
_____
_____
_____
_____
_____

Exercise 2: Tuning into Your Inner Guidance

Practise tuning into your inner guidance by engaging in meditation or quiet reflection. Ask yourself questions related to your desires and listen for intuitive nudges or insights. Pay attention to any inspired ideas or actions that arise from this practice.

_____
_____
_____
_____
_____
_____
_____
_____
_____
_____
_____
_____
_____
_____
_____
_____

Exercise 3: Creating Your Plan of Action

Create a plan of action that outlines the key steps you need to take in order to manifest your desires. Break down these steps into smaller, manageable tasks and assign timelines to each. Ensure that each action is aligned with your intentions and that it feels inspiring and in alignment with your true desires.

_____

_____

_____

_____

_____

_____

_____

_____

_____

_____

_____

_____

_____

_____

_____

WEEK 6: EXERCISES

Exercise 1: Exploring Limiting Beliefs

Take some time to reflect on any limiting beliefs that may be blocking your manifestations. Write them down in your manifestation journal and then challenge each belief by providing evidence to the contrary. Replace these limiting beliefs with empowering affirmations.

_____
_____
_____
_____
_____
_____
_____
_____
_____
_____
_____
_____
_____
_____

Exercise 2: Building Trust and Patience

Engage in activities that cultivate trust and patience within you. Practise meditation or visualisation exercises to strengthen your faith in the manifestation process. Write down affirmations that reinforce your trust and patience and read them daily.

_____

_____

_____

_____

_____

_____

_____

_____

_____

_____

_____

_____

_____

_____

_____

_____

Exercise 3: Creating Your Resilience Practice

Design a resilience practice that aligns with your needs and preferences. This can include activities like exercise, mindfulness, gratitude or any other practices that help you cultivate resilience. Integrate this practice into your daily routine.

_____

_____

_____

_____

_____

_____

_____

_____

_____

_____

_____

_____

_____

_____

_____

Exercise 4: Self-Study Reflection and Planning

Allocate dedicated time for self-reflection and planning. Set aside uninterrupted moments to review the course material, engage in journaling exercises, and plan your ongoing self-study journey. Consider how you will incorporate the lessons and practices into your daily life.

_____

_____

_____

_____

_____

_____

_____

_____

_____

_____

_____

_____

_____

_____

_____

www.ingramcontent.com/pod-product-compliance
Lightning Source LLC
Chambersburg PA
CBHW052203110526
44591CB00012B/2055